MYTHS
AND
LEGENDS
OF
IRELAND

MYTHS
AND
LEGENDS
OF
IRELAND

RONALD PEARSALL

SMITHMARK

This edition published in 1996 by SMITHMARK Publishers, a division of U.S. Media
Holdings, Inc., 16 East 32nd Street, New York, NY 10016.

SMITHMARK books are available for bulk purchase for sales promotion and premium use.
For details write or call the manager of special sales, SMITHMARK Publishers, 16 East 32nd
Street, New York, NY 10016; (212) 532-6600

This book was designed and produced by
Todtri Productions Limited
P.O. Box 572
New York, NY 10116-0572
Fax (212) 279-1241

Printed and bound in Singapore

Library of Congress Catalogue Number 95-072409

ISBN 0-8317-6232-2

Author: Ronald Pearsall

Publisher: Robert M. Tod
Designer and Art Director: Ron Pickless
Editor: Nicolas Wright
Typeset and DTP: Blanc Verso/UK

CONTENTS

INTRODUCTION

The mythology of Ireland is unlike that of any other. In its diversity and variety it has no equal. The mythologies of ancient Greece were codified by the great writers of the time; there is no question what Ulysses did or did not do. Homer tells us, and who are we to argue? Sir Thomas Malory introduced order into English mythology, though many elements were probably brought in from Ireland and Wales.

But the myths and legends of Ireland were oral, handed down over the centuries, altered and amended, sometimes to fit in with the Christian beliefs, sometimes on the whim of the travelling story-tellers, and were not put into written form until the eleventh century and after.

Ireland is immutable; it does not change, and most of it has not changed. A Celtic warrior could be deposited in its midst and be convinced that he was in his own time. Ireland largely escaped the Industrial Revolution; there are few tracts of desolate wasteland. The entire population is no more than about five million, considerably less than either London or New York.

The mythology is violent and tender in turn. It can be fragmentary, and hallucinatory vivid. Who can forget the image of three hanging naked women, largely unexplained? Or the beautiful story of the four maidens turned into swans and doomed to their fate for hundreds of years? Or the hideous hags who are transmuted by love into beautiful women? Or the ghastly horror of the shrinking hut?

Some of the stories are not for the faint-hearted. But there are others, compassionate and benign, that show a different side of the ancient Celtic culture, a culture that lives on indifferent to what has been called progress.

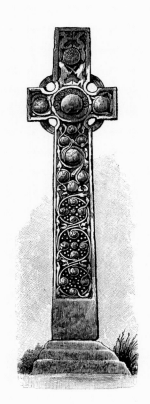

MYTHOLOGY
THE REASON WHY

Mythology is the ancestral memory of a race of people, modified, embroidered, and filtered through a variety of sources, so much so that it emerges as confusing, contradictory, and often utterly bewildering until we take stock of it.

Until we forget that we are in the final years of the twentieth century and try to project ourselves back thousands of years. Then it all becomes clear; we know the reason for the mythology, and what started it, and if we are persistent we can unravel the tangled skeins until it makes sense.

Even in the case of Irish mythology which is one of the most complex and ornate of them all.

Bronze Age men and women (from 3500 BC) and Iron Age men and women (from 2000 BC) – though the dates in Ireland were considerably later – were not, as was often supposed, savages. In mental capacity they were our equal. If we take the Iron Age and then consider today, we realise that almost exactly in the middle of this span of years came the Greek and Roman civilizations. If their culture was not the equal of ours, then you should read no further.

These ancient peoples of the Bronze Age and the Iron Age, recently skilled in the use of these metals, lived a day-to-day existence, dependent on the climate, the sun, the vagaries of nature. If the weather was harsh they starved, in the winter when there was little sun they sought what shelter there was from the elements, and it was natural for them to regard nature with awe, and personify the various phenomena. The sun was benevolent; it ripened their crops and it made life easier, and it was natural, not knowing what the sun was, whether it was a few miles away or an immeasurable distance, to treat it as a god, a god with human attributes.

This was true of the moon, the mysterious stars, thunder and lightning, the rain which Ireland is so rich in, and the wind. All were given names and qualities, or sometimes they were regarded as different moods of the sun, which, in the manner of all gods from whatever part of the world, could change its appearance at will.

It was often believed that the sun changed its attitude towards its minions because it had been offended in some way, and

Emblematic of the Ireland of legend, its mystery and its beauty, Gallarus Oratory in County Kerry, eerily solitary and calm.

Above:
The entrance and passageway of an ancient Celtic cairn, with the passage oriented to the sunrise of the winter solstice, and the stones richly adorned with Celtic ornamentation.

Right:
Triple goddesses, often believed to control the weather, the fertility of the land, or the destinies of the people.

Above: The evil queen Medb, possessed of supernatural attributes, drawn by a strange cat-like creatures in her chariot.

Left: Iona Cathedral on the Island of Iona in the Inner Hebrides, Scotland, stands on the site of a monastery founded by St. Columbia who arrived there from Ireland in AD 563.

therefore it had to be propitiated by ceremonies. These could vary from place to place, ranging from the most modest of entreaties to human sacrifice. Sometimes these failed to work, and new methods were used. It was sometimes necessary to fabricate new gods who would take on the power of the sun or attempt to placate or trick it in some way or other. Or gods could be renamed and even well-established gods with unique characteristics could, if the circumstances dictated, turn out to be the same ones under an alias, which was often never disclosed to their susceptible subjects.

Consequently there arose people who had a special gift for dealing with these unknown forces, and throughout recorded time they were regarded with reverence, and credited with immense powers. Some of them are still with us in the guise of witch-doctors in Africa.

Throughout history we have these wise men; in Arthurian legend we have the wizard Merlin, and amongst the Celts especially in Ireland, we have the professional scholars, the learned monks, and the Druids, who have never been treated with the importance they merit.

As time went by, genuine history and mythology became mixed, mythological figures became real people, and heroes became gods. Without a written language – a deliberate choice as the wise men insisted on their traditions being handed down orally – this was unavoidable, and each generation added something or changed the emphasis. Without a written language, names became jumbled or interchangeable, especially vaguely

Ronwe.

Previous page:
A dramatic skyscape, Loughkeelan, County Down. The moods of the climate were regarded as reflections of the gods' temperament.

Left:
One of the irrational creatures of myth, symbolic of "the silly, savage and senseless element" in myth and its dieties and harbingers.

similar as the Celts in Wales, Ireland, Britain, north-west France and Scotland spoke a similar but not indentical language. There became an increasing desire to make sense of it all.

We can therefore divide myths into the rational and the irrational, and these are not only the myths of the Celtic world but of those throughout the world, including Greece and Rome where reason by and large held sway.

The rational myths are those which present gods as beautiful and wise spirits, typical of these being the Greek Artemis of the Odyssey, "taking her pastime in the chase of boars and swift deer, while with her the wild wood-nymphs disport them, and high over them all she rears her brow, and is easily to be known where all are fair". This is a charming picture, all a god of nature should be. But there is another Artemis co-existing, who could be a she-bear or a star, just as the majestic Zeus could also be at the same time a rapist, a trickster, and a thoroughly unpleasant character.

One authority of the nineteenth century, the Anglo-German academic Max Müller (1823-1900), was very disapproving of what he termed "the silly, savage and senseless element" in myths, and tried to explain it away by theories that there had

Top right:
Fearful of the Underworld, the ancient peoples of Ireland tried to propitiate and please its gods. Only later was the Otherworld transformed into a place of happiness and joy.

Below right:
Lightning and thunder were often regarded as manifestations of the sun-god's rage, leading to horror and bloody murder.

been some kind of pollution in the language, some major misunderstanding, that it was so complicated that only he and his colleagues could even begin to understand it.

His ideas, innovative as they were, are little regarded today, but when they were first put out they were seriously considered, and it made mythology even more of a puzzle, especially when the languages of Sanskrit, Egyptian and Babylonian had only recently been broken down and the mythologies of these countries was not only incomprehensible because of the communication barrier, but even when the language barrier was conquered difficult to understand anyway.

The Greeks and the Romans were themselves perplexed by their own more extravagant and monstrous myths, and tried to distance themselves from the more distasteful by pretending that they were allegorical and needed analysis before they could be understood, which of course was ideal for wise men and prophetesses such as Cassandra. The manner is which gods changed their shapes with annoying regularity was explained by the Egyptians; in moments of danger, gods changed their shapes to fool their antagonists.

As early as 316 BC the writer Euemerus maintained that myths are history in disguise, and that all the gods were once men

Above:
The holy wells of Ireland are still regarded with reverence and awe, and many go great distances to visit them

Previous page:
Myths, wrote Eurmerus in 316 BC, were history in disguise, but what were the early inhabitants of Ireland to make of the Giant's Causeway in County Antrim? They believed the 'pathway' of hexagonal columns to have been built by giants, or used by giants to walk to Scotland.

Right:
The ancient Piper Stones of County Wicklow which predated many of the "five invasions" of Ireland, and which would have struck the new arrivals with awe and incomprehension - sentiments which are still with us

Many of the earliest races of mythological Ireland are half-human half-supernatural, such as the Famorians, embodying the spirit of evil.

whose feats had been decorated and distorted through the generations. This theory was greatly to the liking of St Augustine and the early Christian writers, and it was revived in the seventeenth century by philosophers, noticing that there were some myths that had a startling resemblance to passages in the Bible. They considered that myths were a distorted form of an original revelation, the Bible a pure version. One French abbé in 1738 went so far as to systematically resolve all the Greek myths, wild and wonderful as many of them were, into ordinary history, no easy task.

In fact, the great enemy to the understanding of mythology were the writers on mythology, who, scholarly and with dedication, pursued their own furrows, disregarding commonsense and creating mystery where there was none. There was a good deal of discussion about whether primitive races had the same thought processes as modern man, whether, as they put it, there was "a period of temporary madness through which the human mind had to pass, and was it a madness identically the same in the south of India and the north of Iceland?"

Why did certain trees have red flowers? Why were some birds black and others white? Why did some deer have antlers and others not? All these were questions that needed asking. And there was always someone who would try and answer them.

Early academics and anthropologists working amongst the native peoples of Africa and the "red men of the American continent" were mostly unable to separate their studies from the rascist attitudes of the time. But Max Müller, who carried out much of this research, was able to make one or two persuasive comments about the stages of myth-making. The "savage" needs to know the "reason why".

What was the origin of the world, and of men, and of beasts? How came the arrangement of the stars and why do they move around? How are the movements of the sun and the moon to be accounted for? Why did a certain tree have red flowers, and why were some birds black and some white? There was such an eagerness to find out the answers to these questions that there was always someone ostensibly wiser than the rest who would supply them, and even the most ludicrous theories were given considerable thought until they were rejected in favour of something better – "world myths". The simplest of these was that the sun was a great god.

There was intense interest in the way the same myths were

The Bocan stone circle at Inishowen, County Donegal. Stone circles are spread throughout the Celtic world - in Great Britain, Ireland, and Brittany. No-one has given a satisfactory explanation for them. Probably no-one ever will.

spread throughout the world, and notions of hazardous journeys of exploration were debated. The simple answer, of course, is that mankind everywhere observed the heavens with awe, and it is not surprising that the most common myth is worship of the sun. There may be civilizations which are ahead of others (just as the Chinese was when the western world was in the throes of the Dark Ages) but there is no question that all cultures have passed through the phase when little makes sense and what does is often terrifying.

Another common myth is the strange concept of death. Natural death was simply not believed in; when someone died it was automatically assumed that he or she was the victim of some supernatural plot, had failed to make the requisite rites, or had somehow incurred the wrath of the gods.

Naturally enough some of the myths were not thrown out, simply because there was nothing better to put in their place. Some of them were startlingly bizarre. The aborigines in Australia thought that the wild dog, the dingo, had the power of human speech; peasants from Britanny (which had much the same historical background as Ireland, a country to which the ancient Celts had fled) credited all birds with language which they claimed to be able to interpret; the Mexicans believed that pregnant women would turn into beasts and sleeping children into mice if certain rituals were not carried through. These theories were held often over many centuries and refutal was impossible, but before we scorn other ancient and modern races they

Spring Pelting Away Winter. The picture is by Calderon, a Victorian artist, but even as late as the nineteenth century its symbolism would have been as clear as the notion was to the early inhabitants of Ireland, with spring embodied as a young maiden and winter as an old hag.

would surely regard our superstitions about walking under ladders and the number thirteen with the same incredulity. Superstition and mythology are inextricably linked.

Primitive people were fearful, and every object, animate or inanimate could arouse dread. They wanted protection from the malevolent forces which they saw all around them, and they were never quite certain what was evil and what was not, whether the smiling sun would turn into a hailing gale with thunder and lightning. So they turned to one of their own who was braver and bolder than they were, who had proved himself in battle, and thus began the hero-worship which is a characteristic feature of mythology.

When all communication was by word of mouth, travelling story-tellers, whatever they were called, were greatly in demand, and have been until very recently. As it was their business, the story-tellers, while claiming to be giving fact, gave their audiences what they wanted to hear – tales of daring-do and heroism not of this world, together with horror stories, the "silly, savage and senseless" elements so denounced by the learned professors. And they were open in admitting this; a story-teller who could not make a coherent tale by taking bits from this legend and bits from that was no true poet.

With so many story-tellers going their separate ways it is not surprising that in mythology there are masses of contradictions and confusion, and there would be more when Christianity arrived in the Celtic world and there was a need to tone down the more extreme material and somehow fit the new faith into the old setting.

Some of the chaos that characterizes Irish mythology disappeared with the arrival of the Romans in Britain. They merely dipped their toes into the strange ocean that was Ireland, though they occupied Wales and there was constant traffic between Wales and Ireland, so much so that many of the myths are interchangeable. The Romans brought with them qualities that were quite new – a written universal language, Latin, and dispassionate observation, though some was more dispassionate than others. One writer (Strabo) held that the inhabitants were addicted to cannibalism and had no marriage ties, another (Solinus) wrote of the luxuriant pastures, but complained that the people were inhospitable and warlike, and that when a male child is born he was fed by tit-bits placed in his mouth on the tip of the father's sword.

The most pedantic commentator was Ptolemy, who recorded the names of sixteen different peoples or tribes, many of them confirmed from other sources. But the most valuable is Tacitus, the Roman historian, who in the second century AD noticed the manner in which traditions were shared between Ireland and the mainland of Britain.

No doubt the Romans could have over-run Ireland had they wished, and unquestionably exploratory visits were made, particularly from Wales which they had occupied without difficulty, but conquering and occupying are two different things as many other nations found throughout Ireland's checkered history.

THE
INVASION
MYTHS

The myths were handed down from generation to generation often in the guise of history. The language was Irish, the third oldest in the western world after Greek and Latin, which spread into Scotland and Wales, and often further afield.

The time when the epic events of Irish mythology took place is vague. Many of the writers are obscure, and the poems by Maelmura (died 884), Cinaed Uah Artacáin (died 975), Eochaid Ua Flainn (died 984), Flann Mainistrech (died 1056) and Gilla Coemgin (died 1072), give intriguing glimpses into the subterranean wealth of Irish legend. Very significant is the *Lebor Gabála* or *Book of Invasions*, which first appeared in a twelfth-century manuscript. It is chronological and there is a sense of order, as though the writer is determined to make sense of a conflicting body of oral evidence.

This tells of successive waves of invaders, and is of immense antiquity though the twelfth-century account was necessarily modified so as to be religiously correct. There is a verve and a vivacity quite on a parallel with the Greek epics.

The first race which inhabited Ireland perished in the Biblical Flood. This is in itself evidence that the Biblical stories have been incorporated into the mythology. 268 years later (for the myth-makers are nothing if not precise) twenty-four men and twenty-four women came to Ireland, led by a character named Partholón (sometimes Partholan) who came from Greece and who landed in what is now County Dublin. At that time there were in Ireland only one treeless and grassless plain, three lakes, and nine rivers, but during Partholón's time four plains and seven new lakes were formed, and agriculture was introduced.

After three centuries the colony had increased to 5000, but the entire population was then wiped out by an epidemic, the people gathering to die on the original plain, being buried at Tamlacht, a word meaning plague-grave (question: if they all died who was there to bury them?)

An extraordinary fact is that excavations have uncovered a number of ancient remains, though they are believed to be Viking. As with all mythology it is possible that later true events have been incorporated in legend.

Although there were no survivors from this plague, the knowledge and skills of the Partholón lived on, though who can say how when there were no writing skills. These included the knowledge and working of gold, the first brewing of beer, and the introduction of domestic cattle. It is possible that later arrivals, always supposing that the entire population was wiped out which commonsense tells us is improbable, saw the physical remains of these enterprises and made their own deductions.

There was also, it seems, a form of law-giving and ritual.

From this legend it would appear that the people of Partholón arrived in an unpopulated desolate land, (again unlikely as Ireland, to say the least of it, is extensive and endlessly fertile), but apparently they were also engaged in fighting the

Above:
The Queen of Tara, the ancient capital of Ireland, the scene of yearly gatherings of all the rulers of Ireland and itself deserted when struck by the plague.

Right:
Aoife bewitching the children of Lir with a magical Druid wand and the chanting of an ancient rune. The illustration is by Helen Stratton for *A Book of Myths* (1915).

Previous page:
To have a mythology, a country must have a nature, a people, a history, a kind of ethos that is sympathetic. So it was in Norway. So it is in Ireland. This is Kilmacduagh, in East Galway.

Fomorians, a race of demons, monstrous and hideous and equipped with supernatural powers, the forces of evil, though other sources simply describe them as sea-pirates. This was the fate also of the next race to invade Ireland, the people of Nemed, a warrior from Scythia who arrived thirty years later with 900 followers ; they cleared twelve new plains and created four new lakes, but they were hit by the same epidemic and were so enfeebled that they were unable to resist the Fomorians and became their slaves. Part of their tribute was the delivery on the first of November of two-thirds of the children born to them each year, and two-thirds of their corn and milk.

The Nemedians destroyed the Fomorian fortress at what is now Tory Island, and joined battle with the Fomorians who, possessed of supernatural powers, or alternatively received reinforcements from Africa, naturally won, and only thirty Nemedian people survived, among them three descendants of Nemed, who set out for different countries. One of them, Simon Brec, went to Greece, and was so prolific that the Greeks became afraid of him and his kin and reduced them to slavery, from which they escaped and returned to Ireland.

A feature of the mythology of this indefinable time is the ease

An early Christian monastery with clochans, Skellig Michael, County Kerry, still a fount of mystery.

34

Mound of the Hostages passage-tomb, Hill of Tara, County Meath, certainly one of the most tantalising sites in the whole of Ireland. Tara represented all that was great and noble about Celtic Ireland.

Right:
The European Celts entering Italy, preparatory to sacking Rome. Only later were they forced to the western extremities of Europe.

with which the various tribes and factions moved around Europe, but the detail is often of help in giving us some kind of rough time scale. The skills of the Partholón people in gold would seem to indicate knowledge of metals.

We are told that Nemed came from Scythia. This is in itself helpful. They were a nomadic tribe inhabiting the steppes north of the Black Sea between the Danube and the Don rivers and flourished between the seventh and second centuries BC. They are known to have extensive trading links with the Persians which indicates a willingness to travel. Perhaps more significant is the fact that the Celts of central Europe occupied for a time this part of the world. In 390 BC the Celts had annihilated the Roman army and sacked Rome.

The next arrivals in Ireland were the Firbolgs together with the less important Fir Gaileoins and Fir Domnanns and they are often grouped together. The Firbolgs had five leaders, each of which occupied a province known as a "fifth", a structure which has remained intact. These provinces were Ulster, Leinster, Connaught, East and West Munster.

The Firbolgs are "real" and descendants of them were described in the Middle Ages as "tattling, guileful, tale-bearing, noisy, contemptible, mean, wretched, unsteady, harsh and

Above:
Carndonagh cross and pillars, County Donegal, of indeterminable age and significance, both to the native population and to the waves of invaders.

Left:
Upright slab combining one large cross, and four smaller ones, with characteristic Celtic circle in the centre, an unusual and sophisticated arrangement, situated at Inishmurray, County Sligo.

Right:
An Anglo-Saxon map of about the ninth century, showing that even then Ireland was at the edge of the known world. It is situated in the bottom left-hand corner entitled Hibernia.

inhospitable". They were soon challenged by the Tuatha Dé Danann (tribes of the god Danu), the forces of light, who were allegedly descended from Nemed, arriving in Ireland via Scandinavia and Scotland. The Tuatha Dé Danaan occupy a peculiar place in this legendary history of Ireland, for while they are treated in one way as ordinary human beings, fighting and winning or losing, they are also supernatural beings, and the story-tellers (known as shanachies) were deliberately ambiguous about them, no doubt shifting the emphasis depending on the audience.

They brought with them the Stone of Destiny (the Lia Fáil – alleged to be the Stone of Scone, part of the throne on which British monarchs are still crowned) which they set up at Tara,

Above:
Intermarriage between the Vikings and the conquered to an extent modified the Celtic race. These were known as the foreign Irish, the Gallgoidel.

Left:
Legananny dolmen, County Down, a feature of all Celtic landscapes from Scotland to Bodmin Moor in Cornwall. The word dolmen was first used in 1849, and is believed to have come from a Cornish word meaning "hole of stone". The word cromlech is also used, especially for the dolmens in Britanny.

Opposite:
Human immolation alleged to have been carried out by the Celts and Druids, though it is
more probable that it was a hate campaign carried out against paganism especially by new
converts to Christianity. There is no evidence
to support such barbarities.

Right:
Yet the Celts were capable of producing
grotesques, such as this head, which may pro-
vide a parallel with the Fomorians, the semi-
human forces of evil.

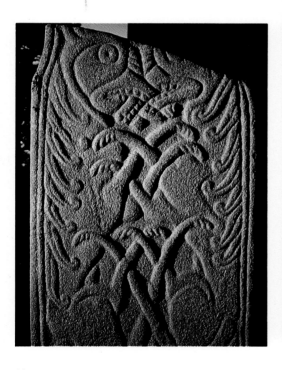

Above:
As with the Romans and the Greeks, fighting
was matched amongst the Irish with intense
artistry. This is a pillar or shaft from
Clonmacnoise, County Offaly, with the most
exquisite of ornamentation.

to be the ancient capital of Ireland. They defeated the Firbolgs
in battle, the defeated Firbolgs being allowed to retain
Connaught, though many fled the country, ending up in
Scotland, particular the Scottish islands.

During the fighting the king of the Tuatha lost his right hand
and because a monarch had to be without physical blemish he
was obliged to abdicate in favour of Bres, the son of a
Fomorian father and a Tuatha mother.

Bres was harsh, imposing severe taxation, and despite dynas-
tic marriages to establish a status quo he was satirised to such
effect by the principal bard of the Tuatha that he came out in
boils and so he too was forced to abdicate, which led to a war
between the Fomorians and the Tuatha with an armoury of
magical weapons, a war which the Tuatha won, the Fomorians
being almost wiped out. For many many years the Tuatha
regime prospered and was unchallenged, and became the gods
of the Irish Celts, eventually retiring, ready to be of service at
some future date, to the prehistoric burial mounds, or fairy

HOW ARTHVR DREW THE SWORD

The legends and myths of old were often interchangeable, and although the legend of Arthur is centred in England, there are grounds for thinking that it may have been instigated or transformed from Welsh or Irish roots. The illustration in which the young Arthur succeeds in drawing the magic sword Excalibur from the stone was executed by H. J. Ford for Andrew Lang's *The Book of Romance* (1902 edition).

From the same source, the magician Merlin is lured to his death in the underground well by Vivien. These mythical events have their counterparts in Irish legend.

mounds, of the country. One of the most important was at New Grange, on the northern bank of the River Boyne. It is a large knoll 280 feet across and forty-four feet high, but, states *The Annals of the Four Masters*, it was plundered by the invading Danes in 861 AD though curious engraved stones survived.

One of the most beautiful of all Irish legends concerns a deity of Tuatha, Lir, the father of the sea-god Mananan who occurs frequently in Irish legend. He had married in succession two sisters, the second one of whom was named Aoife (pronounced Eefa). By an earlier wife Lir had four children, whom he loved, which aroused such jealousy in Aoife that she resolved to put them to death. She journeyed to a neighbouring king, Böv the Red, taking the children with her and by a lonely lake she ordered her attendants to kill them. They refused and rebuked her, so that instead of killing them she used magic to turn them into four white swans, and laid a curse on them. 300 years they would spend on the lake, 300 years they would spend on the

Excalibur, the magical sword, is taken by a
ghostly hand as it is thrown into the Mere.
Taken from Lang's *'The Book of Romance'*.

A kiss between Arthur and Guinevere.
Illustratedby Ford, after Lang's *'The Book of
Romance'*.

Straits of Moyle (between Ireland and Scotland), and 300
years on the Atlantic Ocean. After that the long evil spell is
lifted, but only when "the woman of the South is mated with
the man of the North."

When Aoife arrived at the palace of Böv the Red without the
children, her guilt was apparent, and Böv turned her into a
demon of the air. She fled shrieking and no more was heard of
her. Lir and Böv sought out the swan children, and found that
not only had they human speech but made wonderful music.
People from all over Ireland visited the swans, and for 300
years the swans enjoyed great peace and tranquility.

The time came for the second part of the spell, 300 years in the
Straits of Moyle. Forbidden to land, battered and driven apart
by the wind, their feathers frozen in the cold, the three
youngest were saved by the eldest daughter, who wrapped her
feathers round them to protect them.

For the third part of their trial they took flight to the western

shores of Mayo, and suffered much hardship, but a new wave of invaders had arrived, the Milesians, from whom the future nobles and kings claimed descent, and the swan-children were befriended by a Milesian farmer, Evric, to whom they told their story and who (supposedly) handed it down. They flew to Armagh to seek their father, but found only green mounds, bushes, and nettles. The palace of their father was there, but they could not see it. There was a higher destiny awaiting these seemingly doomed creatures.

They heard for the first time a Christian bell, the sounds coming from the chapel of a hermit, which terrified the swans until reassured by the hermit who indoctrinated them into the ways of Christianity.

Above:
The monks and hermits often lived lonely and desolate lives, at the mercy of not only the local inhabitants but of the invaders and marauders.

Left:
How a Celtic settlement would have appeared. This is the imaginative Craggaunowen project, County Clare.

Left:
Dramatic traces of Irish heritage can be seen, seemingly, everywhere.

Right:
The coming of Christianity meant that Bible stories were incorporated into traditional mythology. Some of them, such as *Death on a Pale Horse*, here illustrated by the French artist Gustave Doré, were not so different from Irish legend.

Deoca, a princess of Munster, the woman of the South in the spell put upon the swan-children, was betrothed to a prince from Connaught, the man of the North, and begged to have the famous four swans as a wedding gift. The hermit, who had linked the swans by silver chains, refused to give them up, but the prince dragged them off. The curse had reached its peak. The woman of the South had met the man of the North.

The swan plumage fell off, they were no longer lovely swans but four white-haired withered and terrible-looking hags. The prince flew in horror from these apparitions, and, as the old women clearly had little time to live, the hermit came and prepared to baptise them.

Fionuala requested that they be buried in one grave, laid in the position in which she had protected the younger children during the years in the straits. This was done, and they went to heaven. The hermit sorrowed for them until the end of his days.

Unquestionably it is one of the most tender and moving of the Irish myths, and introduces the new race, the Milesians, who

Left:
The arrival of the Vikings. Sometimes they came to slaughter, sometimes they came as benevolent conquerers, but they changed the face of Celtic Ireland as the Normans were to do even more thoroughly centuries later.

Right:
A Celtic shield. Notice the curling pattern so typical of the Irish culture, revived in Ireland and Britain in the art nouveau period in the late nineteenth century.

The Milesians are particularly interesting as they are represented in much Irish legend as wholly human. And the Tuatha are not truly defeated, because by their magic arts they confer invisibility on themselves, which they can put on or off as they please. Henceforward, there are two Irelands, the spiritual and the earthly. Some commentators offer the theory that the Milesians were "evolved" because of Christianity, that Tuatha was irretrievably pagan, a new regime not much different from the old was called for, and a regime that was human (for otherwise there would be no point in promoting Christianity).

The two Milesian brothers who had divided the land between them battled for control of all-Ireland, and one of them was killed. Eventually, the Milesians were overthrown by the subject peoples led by Cairbre Cinnchait ("cat-head") in AD 90, though apparently their rule was later restored.

Thus the history of Ireland according to *The Book of Invasions*.

This book is complemented, sometimes contradicted, by other material of the time. Of the chronicles perhaps *The Annals of Ulster* which deals with that province from the year 441 AD is one of the most valuable and explicit, though there are such compilations as *The Book of Rights* and lengthy epics such as *Táin Bo Cualnge* which have to be taken into account.

Prior to the Tuatha Dé Danann it is not possible to find out with any certainty any facts at all; Partholón may be the leader of a group, or may represent an entire tribe. The references to Ireland being a desolate plain with no trees is utterly incomprehensible, unless Partholón is viewed as a fertility god who caused the land to bloom. Because the real history of Ireland involves almost continuous fighting, it was easy enough for the myth-makers to incorporate this in their world picture.

Amongst the Firbolg, who undoubtedly were a distinct race, their king Eochaid mac Eire seems to have been some sort of benevolent father-figure, and in his time Ireland was briefly a land of happiness and content, perhaps as a result of his marriage with Tailtiu, an earth goddess, a further fertility symbol. Only with the Tuatha Dé Danann do the gods and goddesses become specific.

The Dagda was the lord of all knowledge, father of all, and was pictured as gross and ugly, pot-bellied and peasant-like, wearing the working-man's dress of tunic and hood, with rawhide sandals on his feet. Whatever his inadequacies in the matter of good looks he made up for it elsewhere. He had a club so large that it would have needed eight men to carry it and it was therefore mounted on wheels. When hauled along the ground it left a ditch, and under his club "the bones of his

Right:
Stone at Rossie Priory, near the old castle of Moncur near Arbroath. This is perhaps a sign of slaughter in Ulster in 729, recounted in *The Annals of Ulster*.

Below:
The sea-god Mananan and two hand-maidens or sub-goddesses.

enemies were like hailstones under horses' hooves". With one end of the club he could kill nine men at a time and with the other restore them to life.

Besides this miraculous club he also possessed a cauldron which never could be emptied, and from which nobody went away unsatisfied. He was therefore a god of fertility, and the cauldron or its mythological equivalents feature strongly in many ancient legends. There is the cow which yields unlimited quantities of milk. It is all to do with the bountiful source which cannot be emptied, and can be seen as a kind of wish-fulfilment when there was not enough food in the pot or the cows had dried up.

When the Tuatha were under the domination of the Fomorians the Dagda showed his ability to build fortresses. On the first of November each year he was obliged to undergo a ritual – eating a huge meal of porridge from out of a hole in the ground, followed, if he could make it no doubt, by sexual inter-course with one of the Fomorian girls. Offerings in pits, whether in the form of porridge or whatever, was a characteris-tic feature in European myth, and the Dagda had his counter-parts elsewhere. Peasant he may seem and gross may be his appetites, but he was also a skilled harpist, able to evoke the seasons of the Celtic year, reinforcing his abilities as a fertility god of great potency.

The god Lug, also known as Lámfhada (of the long arm) or Samildánach (many skilled), had many of the Dagda's func-

The so-called Tara brooch, found by a peasant woman in Drogheda in 1850, of rare intricacy and craftsmanship.

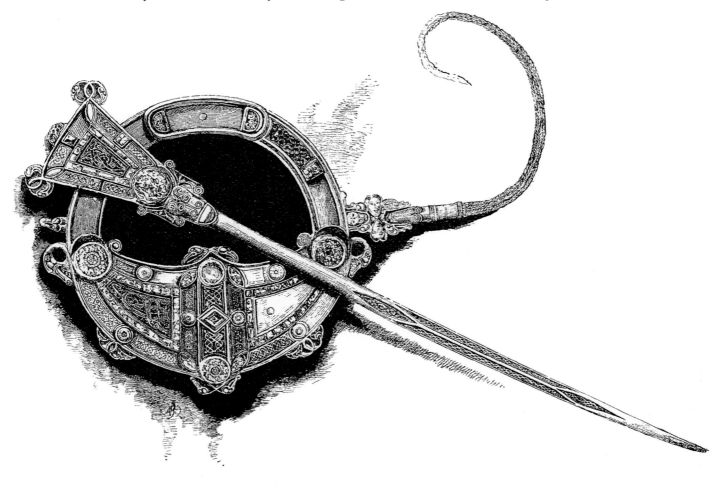

tions. When he arrived to join the Tuatha Lug was asked by the guard at the gate of the royal palace of Tara what was his trade. He replied that he was a carpenter. On being told that the Tuatha had a carpenter he said he was a smith. There was no vacancy for a smith, nor for the other trades Lug pronounced himself skilled in – a warrior, a harpist, a poet, a hero, a magician, and so on. But when the guard was asked if they had anyone skilled in all of them the guard had to confess they had not, so Lug was admitted. Unlike the Dagda, with whom he may or may not have co-existed, Lug was handsome, armed with a spear and sling with which he could hurl missiles at an amazing distance. With his sling he took out the single eye of Balor, the champion of the Fomorians, and thus became a hero.

He was probably as important as any other god in Irish mythology, and his fame extended over the seas to France where there were at least fourteen Gallic towns named after him, one of which gradually changed its name to Lyons. He was certainly a sun god; the shining of his face and brow

The four swan-children in one of the most moving and tender of Irish sagas.

were as bright as the sun on a summer's day, and when Bres wondered why the sun was rising in the west the Druids explained that this was the splendour of Lug. The "red colour was on him from sunset to morning". The rising of the sun in the west and the setting in the east was one of the great mysteries of the ancient world, and remained so until the age of Galileo and Copernicus.

Lug was also the god of lightning, and his spear was a symbol of this as was his secondary name, "of the long arm". Of his spear it was said that when battle was near it was drawn out, it roared and struggled against its thongs and fire flashed from it.

Other gods are less easily categorized. Nuada, part god, part king, is an indistinct figure who lost his hand in battle and had it replaced by a silver one. He had a sword which unsheathed was so powerful that no-one could escape it, a legend uncannily reminiscent of King Arthur's sword Excalibur. Many authorities believe that the King Arthur legend originated in Ireland.

Despite this sword Nuada was killed fighting the new super-race, the Milesians. Many of the gods were specialists, brewers of beer, smiths, champions who fought the ruler's individual enemies (a role that existed in the British monarchy until recent times), and, generally speaking, craftsmen-gods occupying a fairly minor role. They can hardly be called hero-figures, and they may well have been "fillers" for the story-tellers when they were ad libbing, creatures of no importance or of no existence except for that specific time and place.

THE HEROIC AND MAGIC MYTHS

The supreme hero-figure of Ulster, the most important of the provinces, was Cú Chulainn, often
known as Cuchulinn (which will be the spelling
used throughout), who was either the son of Lug,
the reincarnation of Lug, or was born three times.
In an event prominent throughout Irish sources, the Cattle-Raid
of Cualgne , the intense heat generated by his body melted the
snow around him for thirty feet. There is a mass of physical
detail about him. He had three crowns of hair, brown, crimson,
and, on top, gold, which fell down between his shoulders. The
Celts had a habit of smearing their hair with a thick wash of
lime, which perhaps explains the origins of the colour variation
in the hero's hair.

In everyday life, he had seven pupils in each eye, seven fingers
on each hand and seven toes on each foot. He wore rich jew-
ellery, a hundred ornaments on his breast. Most spectacular were
his contortions when a battle was looming, where everything
quivered and his body became deformed; his knees, shins,and
feet shifted themselves until they were behind him. His face
became transformed; one eye became engulfed in the head, the
other rested on his cheek, an inexplicable sign, the "hero's

Previous page:
The Bocan stone circle, Inishowen, County
Donegal, seen at its most awe-inspiring
under a full moon.

Right:
Thomastown Castle, County Tipperary, a
reminder of the distant times when the
under-kings needed to be constantly on their
guard against insurrection or the adventures
of other tribal leaders.

Below:
Celtic legend and history, whether it
relates to Ireland, Great Britain or the other
ancient heartlands, has its heroic queens, none
more famous and brave than Boadicia, the
statue of whom is situated at the north end of
Westminster Bridge, London, atop her
scythe-wheeled chariot.

Above:
Gods and goddesses had the power to transform themselves into whatever they wished, including the form of a monstrous dragon.

Left:
The cliffs of Moher with O'Brien's Tower, County Clare. Brien, sometimes known as Brian or Bran, was one of the great hero-figures of Ireland, and acquitted himself with great courage at the battle of Clontarf, where he was killed.

moon", appeared on his cheek, he breathed out fire, and his heart-beat was like a lion charging bears. This must have been a late gloss, as no-one in Ireland could have expected to have encountered lions or known what they were, even in the earliest of times.

When he was in this state, Cuchulinn had to be plunged three times in a vat of water to pacify him, though there are no records of exactly when this took place throughout the transformation. It must have been an operation fraught with peril.

His hair became entangled and resembled a thorny bush, but the most spectacular event was the jet of dusky blood which shot out of his scalp "longer than the mast of a great ship". This turned into a mist, and finally Cuchulinn leapt into a chariot with scythes on the wheels and drove off, delivering hundreds of "thunder feats". This is the personification of natural phenomena carried to its ultimate. The benevolent sun turning into an incomprehensible thunder cloud flashing lightning.

Unlike many other mythological figures, he had an established human identity, child of a high-born Celt, sent away – as was the custom – to foster parents, and rigorously educated for a special role in society, with an emphasis on magic and sorcery. As was customary, he made his debut as a hero in battle. Although invincible, was able to defend Ulster single-handed against the other four provinces, he was severely wounded on several occasions, as gods had to experience mortal pain or their prestige would be lowered.

His exploits are many, and one of the most interesting and strangest takes place when he lay asleep against a pillar-stone after hunting, and had a vision of two women who came to him armed with rods and one after the other beat him until he was almost dead. He was ill for a year, and then a stranger came to him and told him to go to the stone where he had had the vision. There he found one of the women who had beaten him dressed in a green mantle who told him that Fand, the Pearl of Beauty, wife of Mananan the sea god, had "set her love on him". She was at war with her husband, her realm was besieged by three demon kings, and Cuchulinn's help was sought. The reward would be the love of Fand.

Cuchulinn sent the charioteer Laeg to report on Fand, and Laeg entered Fairyland, which lay beyond a lake which he crossed in a magic boat of bronze. He returned to Cuchulinn with tales of Fand's beauty and the glories of Fairyland, and so the hero went off, was involved in a fierce battle in a dense mist with demons who resembled sea waves (presumably the minions of the sea god), triumphed, and stayed with Fand for a month, making a tryst at the Strand of the Yew Tree on earth.

However, his wife Emer heard of the tryst, and although he was noted for his infidelities she decided that she had had enough, and at the trysting place Cuchulinn and Fand were approached by Emer and fifty of her maidens, with gold clasps on their breasts, armed with knives to slay Fand.

Cuchulinn addresses Emer in a curious poem, describing the beauty and magical powers of Fand, and Emer laments that she

Diarmid Seizes The Giant's Club

Left:
Diarmid, fighting with the giant and seizing his club.

Overleaf:
Floating between water and sky – an evocative view of Dunguaire Castle County Galway

Below:
A vivid re-enactment of the exploits of Cuchulinn, though, alas, the participants were unable to spout a jet of blood from the top of their heads or turn their legs the wrong way round.

herself seems to have lost the power to attract him – "Once we dwelled in honour together and still might dwell if I could find favour in thy sight."

Cuchulinn has qualms, Fand realises that Emer has natural justice on her side, and asks him to go back to Emer and give her up. But Emer intervenes, and offers to give her husband up to Fand. Fand departs, despite the shame of being rejected, but she is then invited by Mananan, the sea god, to go with him. She retorted "Neither of ye is better or nobler than the other, but I will go with thee, Mananan, for thou hast no other mate worthy of thee, but that Cuchulinn has in Emer."

Cuchulinn had not observed any of this, but was told of the arrangement by Laeg, the charioteer, upon which he bounded into the air and fled the place, lay for a long time refusing food or drink, and was then given a draught of forgetfulness by the Druids. Mananan, who seems to have been one of the more powerful gods, shook his cloak between Cuchulinn and Fand so that they might meet no more throughout eternity. The cloak symbolises the dividing and estranging powers of the sea.

It was essential for heroes to die unconquered and without descendants, and when Cuchulinn's time came to die it was through supernatural means, in this case the machinations of the evil Queen Medb, who had trained many sorcerers as part of a long-term plan to bring Cuchulinn down. Ritual acts, known as

geisa (singular – geis), were part of everyday life, and to omit them was to incur trouble. The more complicated a life, such as the one led by Cuchulinn, where it was not just a question of hoping for a good harvest, the more the ritual acts accumulated.

It was Cuchulinn's misfortune to pass a hearth where three of Medb's sorceresses were roasting a dog at a hearth. When passing a hearth it was essential to taste the food, which he did, but another geis was not to eat dog, and as he ate a shoulder of dog his powers were diminished, not sufficiently to destroy him absolutely but to leave him vulnerable. Demands were then made upon him by a poet, but the demands were refused, even though the poet threatened to satirise him. This was a potent threat, and had the further effect of weakening Cuchulinn, until he fell, mortally wounded.

Early in his career as a hero he had been obliged to kill a guard dog. It had been foretold that his first and last acts would be the killing of a dog. As he washed off the blood from his curious encounter with the poet (satire rarely draws actual blood) he killed an otter (or river-dog) which came to drink from the stream. In his death agony he bound himself to a pillar and defied his enemies until the end, so dying with his honour intact.

Despite everything, Cuchulinn seems to have been a local rather than a universal hero, a defender of Ulster against all comers, natural or supernatural. Finn was conceived as less local, one of the band of the Fiana (sometimes spelled Fianna), the young warrior troops of the kind that permeated mythologies ancient and modern, from the knights of King Arthur's Round Table to the valiant and doomed heroes of the American Western.

The Fiana were not gods, but neither were they ordinary human beings, being possessed of supernormal powers and often in contact with the otherworld that meant so much to the ancient peoples. Finn in fact lived until he was 230. Unlike other figures in mythology he is a genuine historical figure.

The Fiana were mercenaries, who had disdained the traditional tribal life, to hunt and fight. They were envied by the ordinary folk who only wished that they had the spirit to follow suit and were conscious that in the warrior-oriented society they were sadly lacking. Their constant presence in the myth-tellers' repertoire was not surprising.

The Fiana were given credit for various enterprises, such as defending Ireland against the Norse attacks, in which they signally failed. There is a good deal of evidence, though, that, in their purely human capacity, they indulged themselves in attacks on Britain under the Romans.

It is a curious feature of writers on Irish mythology that some give emphasis to certain heroes/gods while almost completely neglecting others who are given extensive coverage by other writers. One possible reason is, as already mentioned, that the same gods turn up under totally different names.

The reason for some of the divergent names is simple enough; the oral myths were transcribed at different times by different people with their own specific linguistic peculiarities. Sometimes there is an honest doubt as to where the myths originated; some could have come from any part of the "traditional" Celtic world, comprising Ireland, Wales – where Finn, meaning white, is Glynn – Scotland, the south west of England, and Britanny, from anywhere where the Celts were based or to where they were forced to flee from stronger invading forces.

The Irish goddesses are largely obscure and lack the charisma of their male counterparts (the various evil queens are more often heard about). They are basically mother-goddesses of the kind that feature in all mythology, and are often confused with each other. There are also language problems. The gods of the Celts are frequently called the people of the goddess Danu, but this does not imply that she gave birth to them. The Dagda was referred to as her father, but this does not mean that he was really her father. Danu also carried the names Anu or Anna, and may have been a triple-goddess (if that concept makes any sense). Similarly Brigit often bore further names, though her most important role is as "ancestor" of St Brigid. Sometimes it seems that Brigit and Danu are the same.

Macha, an Ulster goddess, was the wife of Nemed, one of the mythological invaders, though alternatively she was the wife of a mere peasant. Against her will and although pregnant she was forced to compete in a race with horses, and somewhat surprisingly won, but died giving birth to twins. In the throes of death she put a curse on the warriors of Ulster and for nine generations these warriors were subject to the pangs of childbirth for five days and four nights at times when they were in great peril.

Once again, Macha is one of those deities who appears in contrasting roles in various versions of a basic mother-goddess fertility-symbol myth. She was not just a wife of an invader or a peasant but a warrior queen in her own right, forcing the sons of her enemies to build the fortifications of the capital of Ulster, Emain Macha. Macha thus joins the pantheon of women warriors such as Boudicca (or Boadicea), queen of the Iceni tribe in Britain, Queen Medb, or the Amazons of classical legend. Macha had supernatural powers and could change her shape, and was often described as being in league with two other warrior goddesses. For a race which spent much of its time fighting, stories of this indomitable trio were no doubt popular.

Unquestionably the early inhabitants of Ireland were a fearless race, and one of the reasons was the existence of an attractive otherworld, the otherworld of fairies, the mounds where the Tuatha rested, the paradise visited by Cuchulinn, the lands described by poets as "The Land under the Waves". "The Land of Youth", or "The Field of Happiness", where everything was perfection, lands rich in food, music, and where love-making and fighting could be indulged in without satiety. All were immortal, wounds accrued in battle healed, and those who were unfortunate enough to get themselves slaughtered were restored to life on the following day. It was attractive enough for men to force or wheedle their way into the otherworld to steal some of the gods' magic treasures, especially the cauldron which never emptied and the cows which gave limitless milk.

Nevertheless it was not an appropriate place for heroes, who by

Above:
The Vikings brought their own gods, formidable rivals to the Celtic pantheon and gradually assimilated. This graphic portrait of Odin, the god of war, is by the nineteenth-century artist Val Prinsep.

Right:
Twelve Pins from Mannin Bay County Galway – a welcoming, tranquil scene that belies the rugged defence of its soaring, majestic cliffs.

Left:
Cromcruac, one of the hideous dragon-like creatures of Celtic legend, the most famous of which was the dragon slain by St. George, the patron saint of England.

Right:
Many of the legends of Ireland are interchangeable with those of other Celtic communities. This one represents a Cornish god condemned to dwell in the mysterious Dozmary Pool (believed at one time to be bottomless) on Bodmin Moor, and who, when he tries to escape, is forced back by supernatural hounds.

their nature have to have something to be heroic about. There was consequently an alternative otherworld, a mirror-image, full of unnamed horrors, demons, and phantoms, the domain of giants with such names as Ysbaddaden, in which heroes would have plenty of opportunity to prove themselves against unlimited ghastliness.

There are curious legends such as the Beheading Game where the participants take it in turn to chop off each others' heads, with few indications whether this is real or, as is common in myth, the heads rejoin the bodies the following day.

More straightforward is the story of the Fomorian king Balor, who was told by the Druids that he would be killed by his grandson. To cancel out this prophecy, Balor had his only child, his infant daughter Ethlinn, imprisoned in a high tower in charge of twelve matrons so that she would be unaware of any sex but her own.

On the mainland were three brothers. One of them, Kian, had a magical cow producing unlimited milk, and Balor determined to

Above:
In legend, heroes were often transformed into animal shape, and often begged to be restored to human form before they died. Wolves, known for their strength, courage and intelligence, were often chosen. They were widespread throughout Ireland, and it is no accident that the classic Irish dog is the wolfhound, a formidable foe to any creature.

Left:
The hero Cuchulinn and Morrigu, who appears in the guise of a talking black carrion crow, the traditional bird of the battlefield in many mythologies.

acquire it, which he did in the guise of a small red-headed boy, sending Kian off on a fool's errand while he stole the cow. Kian revenged himself on Balor by dressing himself in a woman's clothes and with a Druidess named Biróg magically arrived at the high tower, pretending to be two noble ladies cast upon the shore and seeking shelter.

Biróg put the twelve matrons to sleep by magic, and Kian seduced Ethlinn and made her pregnant. The matrons, fearful of the consequences if Balor found out, told Ethlinn it was all a dream. Alas, it was not, and she bore three sons, news of which reached Balor who commanded that the three babies be drowned in a whirlpool off the Irish coast. The messenger rolled up the children in a sheet, but the pin of the sheet came out and one of the children fell into a bay, known to this day as Port na Delig, the Haven of the Pin. The other two children drowned, but the Druidess wafted the saved baby to Kian, the father. The child eventually grew up to be Lug, the god.

Kian is a leading character/hero figure in another story. He is sent north by Lug to summon fighting troops, and on the way he meets a group of brothers who are blood/tribal enemies. He changes himself into a pig, joining a herd rooting for food. One of the brothers detects him, and spears and mortally wounds him. Kian, knowing he is about to die, begs to be allowed to change back into human form before he dies. "I would as soon kill a man as a pig!" says the leader, Brian (known in myth as Bran, Ban, Bron or Bran-dua), and Kian stands before them in human form, blood trickling from his breast, boasting that he had outwitted them, that the eric (blood-fine) of a pig is much less than the eric of a man, especially him, the father of a great god. And the spears will tell the tale to the avenger of blood. So Brian and his companions stone him to death.

When Kian's son Lug passes that way the stones on the plain cry out (a familiar feature in myth) and tell him of the murder. Lug approaches the High King. The murderers can either be executed or a blood-fine will be paid. Lug choses the blood-fine. He demands three apples, the skin of a pig, a spear, a chariot with two horses, seven swine, a hound, a cooking-spit, and finally three shouts on a hill.

The murderers, no doubt thinking that they have got off lightly, and possibly mystified by the array of penalties, agree to pay the fine. But things are not what they seem, as they rarely are in myth. The apples are those which grow in the Garden of the Sun, the pig skin heals all wounds and is difficult to acquire, the spear is a magic spear owned by the King of Persia, the pigs can be eaten every day and are yet whole the next day, the spit belongs to an underwater spirit, and the shouts are to be delivered on the hill of a fierce warrior who with his sons are under a vow to prevent any man raising his voice on the hill.

Any one of these tasks is nearly impossible to accomplish, but the men set about it, nearly manage, return, but then Lug causes forgetfulness to fall on the men and grabs the spoils himself so that he can do magical warfare with the Fomorians. The story is not yet over. Dejected, their blood-fine not completed, and still

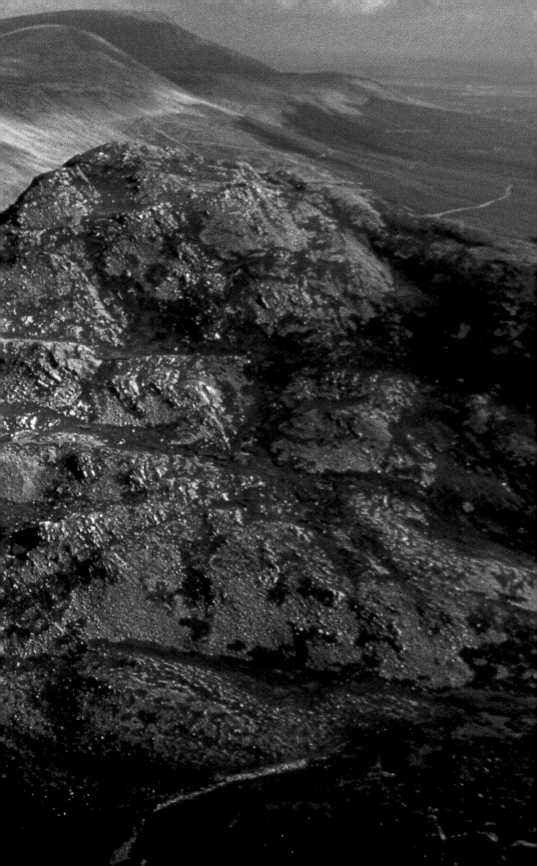

THE DEATH OF DIARMID

Above:
Celtic-Irish chariot and weapons, though the chariot wheels were more often spoked. Wheels for waggons were usually solid.

Left:
The death of the hero Diarmid, who eloped with the future bride of his friend, the great Finn.

Previous page:
The north, from Errigal, County Donegal. With inhospitable terrain such as this, it is hardly surprising that the Irish have succeeded in keeping out those who attempted to complete-ly over- run the country, a task that has never been achieved.

held to it despite the duplicity of Lug, they carry on their task, seize the spit from the underwater kingdom, shout from the hill, being forced to kill the owner and his sons though they too are mortally wounded in the conflict. The blood-fine now paid, hon-our restored, they return, and their aged father begs Lug for the loan of the healing pig-skin to restore them to life, but Lug refus-es and they die, together with the father.

There are myths that explain place names. The River Shannon was named from the goddess Sinend, who went to a magic well under the sea (in the otherworld). She omitted to enact some rit-ual, and the well water surged up and overwhelmed her, wash-ing her on to the shore, where she died, giving to the new river her name.

There are fragmentary myths. In an account of one of the innu-merable battles the warriors on the one side build a cairn, each man contributing one stone, so that there will be a memorial of the fight. The survivors remove one stone each, so that the num-bers of the slain will be known by the amount of the stones left in the cairn. There are spears which have to be kept in a brew of soporific herbs or they will massacre anything in their path (an allusion perhaps to the spear as a symbol of lightning).

There are fantastic creatures such as the three giants from the Isle of Man with horses' manes reaching to their heels. And there are macabre scenes – the three naked and bleeding female forms hanging by ropes from a roof, the daughters of the Bav, another name for the Morrigan, or war-goddess. Their presence is enig-matic: "three of awful boding; those are the three that are slaugh-tered at every time." Every what time? Who can say? What bas-tardized text has this come from?

Transformation scenes abound. Gods, goddesses, heroes, ambiguous characters who may be human, semi-human, or supernatural, change into almost every conceivable shape. Shape-changing was a strong feature of the repertoire of the story-teller. One of the most trenchant, if predictable, is con-tained in the epic *Fitness of Names*.

There is a preamble in which Daire, the father of Curoi, one of the several sun-gods, asks a Druid which of his sons will take the kingdom after he has died. The Druid replies that a fawn with a golden lustre upon it will appear, and the son who catches it will be the successor. The brothers go out to seek the fawn. As is often the case in such parables, the chase is interrupted by strange mists and snow and eventually one of the hunters finds a house, magnificent, with plenty of food, drink and a blazing fire.

There he meets an old women with spears of teeth outside her head and wearing old, foul, and faded clothes. She refuses to give him shelter unless he sleeps with her, and, aghast, he refus-es, as do three other brothers. But Lugaid, one of the brothers, agrees, and when she leads him to the bed she is transformed into a gorgeous maiden in a purple bordered gown.

Afterwards Lugaid fetches his brothers, no doubt somewhat envious, and they eat and drink with the help of "self-moving drinking horns."

There is a variant of this where the sons find the deer near Tara,

kill it, and while resting are approached by a monstrous hag, ugly and bald, as high as a mast, her ear as large as a hut, her front tooth bigger than the square of a chess-board (which might imply a late gloss – chess is difficult to date back in Europe before the eleventh century). The hag was a continuous belly without ribs, and she had a rugged, hilly, block head, set upon the body like a "furzy" mountain. Trying unsuccess-fully to excite their passions, she threatens to turn them into monsters if one of them would not sleep with her. One of them does, and she is transformed into a beauty.

In yet another version of *The Exploits of the Sons of Eochaid Mugmedon*, the five brothers are camping after slaying a boar. One of them, Fiachna, goes to fetch water from a fountain, but on the brink is a sorceress – "A mouth she had into which a hound would fit; the spiked tooth-fence about her head was more hideous than all the goblins of Erin."

It has been speculated that these transfiguration myths are emblematic of the changes of the seasons. And, of course, sexual symbolism has been sought in Irish mythology, a difficult task as the Irish had no difficulty in spelling out sexual activity, and there is a refreshing candour in the absence of prurience. Sex, fighting, the chase, the alliance between humans and the people of the otherworld whether they be demons, gods, tribes who may or may not be superhuman – all these are combined with commentary on the nature of existence, on whether the sun is an individual and why the stars are set in the heavens in that partic-ular configuration. And whether they move of their own volition or forced on their endless round by unseen forces that can only be dimly imagined. Though those too would be defined by someone, a story-teller, a scholar, or a Druid.

There is much that is graphic and lurid about early Irish mythology, but unlike that of Greece and Rome it is disorganized and chaotic, a random mix often without much of the poetry many of the deities professed to be so interested in. In one way this is a delight. It is a distorted reflection of human life, where, seek as we may, there is no pattern, and comedy and tragedy, happiness and sadness, are strung together in a haphazard way. In the personages, human, semi-human, and supernatural, who exist in Irish myth there is a mixture of good and bad qualities, rarely the perfection that graces characters from other mytholo-gies. This often leads to the unexpected, as when a hero behaves in a decidedly unheroic way; an untypical way is understand-able, considering that most Irish legend was not written down until the eleventh century, and pagan stories had to be grafted on to a Christian format. Sometimes the story-tellers had to exert their ingenuity to the full to make a comprehensible narrative, and in doing so what were personal and often wild interpola-tions were taken out of context by their successors until the irrel-evant assumed an importance it did not merit. All writers on the subject must be aware of this, and this applies as well to the readers. They are not reading a novel with a beginning, a mid-dle, and an end, but a stirring compilation of what appealed to a scribe at a random point in time.

Opposite:
The Irish hero Brian defeating the Danish invaders at the Battle of Clontarf, exclaiming to his troops "The blessed Trinity hath at length looked down upon our sufferings, and endued you with the power and the courage, this day, to extirpate for ever the tyranny of the Danes over Ireland; thus punishing them for their innumerable crimes and sacrileges by the avenging power of the sword."

THE FAIRY FOLK

Throughout Irish mythology one of the most consistent features is the existence and pre-eminence of the fairy folk. These are not the coy little Disney-like creatures with wings of children's stories. The name derives from a Latin word meaning enchant, which in turn comes from the Latin *fatum*, fate or destiny. Of all the creatures of mythology, the fairies are the most numerous, the most beautiful and the most memorable in literature. They are spread throughout the world, but those of Ireland have a special interest and unlike many nations, the fairies still exist in their midst.

In Greek mythology the fairy was equated with the nymph, and also the sirens who lured sailors to their doom, so that all is not sweetness and light. They are the Nereids, the Oreads, and the Naiads, the spirits of wells, mountains, and water. In Ireland they dwell in the ancient burial mounds (sometimes called raths), the remains of the fortresses and their earthworks, and in the ruins of buildings erected by the Anglo-Norman invaders in the twelfth century.

They are an organized folk, often called "the army", and their life corresponds to that of humans. They carry off children, substituting changelings in their wake, transport men and women into fairyland, and are regarded as the cause of much supernatural phenomena, even today when poltergeist phenomena is put down to fairy mischievousness. In 1907 in northern Ireland a farmer was troubled with flying stones; his

Previous pages:
Throughout the carnage and supernatural doings of the myths, there is a background of serenity and profundity represented by the traces of men and women beyond the reach of time, as in the Bocan stone circle at Inishowen, County Donegal.

Left:
The sea-god Mananan, one of the most powerful of the supernatural deities.

Right:
The grave of the Reverend Robert Kirk, who wrote a book on fairies and died in 1692. It was believed that he was taken to the Otherworld. He is buried at Aberfoyle, Perthshire, and his book was published by the great novelist, Sir Walter Scott.

Left:
The fairy scribe with a spell-casting fairy, one of the "wee folk." The illustration is by Gordon Wain, 1989, in the collection of Charles Walker.

Right:
Fairies frolicking about a standing stone, beneath which was the Otherworld. Illustration by Gordon Wain, 1991.

neighbours said that the fairies had caused this because he had swept his chimney with a holly bough, and the holly is a "gentle tree" dear to the fairies. When a house became "infested" with fairies the owners left, and the house remained unoccupied.

The fairy marching army raises clouds of dust, and when neolithic arrow-heads and flints are discovered they are assumed to be fairy weapons, are dipped in water and given to ailing animals and people as a remedy for diseases. They often produce mysterious music, in Ireland that of the harp. The author of a book on fairies, the Reverend Mr Kirk, who died in 1692, was published by no less a person than the novelist Sir Walter Scott in 1815. The Scots, too, have a reverence for fairies, second only to their devotion to the phenomenon of second sight. Although Mr Kirk's tomb is, or was, in existence, it was said that he was carried away by fairies. A friend who was told that if he threw a dirk (dagger) over his shoulder Mr Kirk would return to earth. This the friend failed to do.

The otherworld inhabited by the fairies is equivalent to the Hades of the classical writers. A human in the otherworld may not eat, for otherwise he will be trapped there for ever. There is a belief that the existence of fairies can be traced back to pre-historic memories of pigmy races who dwelt in underground earth-houses, and the early races in Ireland were much smaller

The fairies were not necessarily sweet little creatures with wings. Often they could not be differentiated from humans. This is a Victorian representation of sanitised fairies from about 1880.

than those who arrived later, lending a bare vestige of credence. Certainly no pigmy bones have ever been found in Ireland. Mostly fairies are of human stature and cannot be distinguished from mortals except by their actions.

This has led to complications, for throughout Irish mythology there are tales of men falling in love with beautiful women, who turn out to be fairies and disappear.

In later years, when mythologies of all kind were systematically suppressed by the church and a rational society, fairies were turned into something not unlike tourist attractions. The little people became, in Ireland, leprechauns, a word first

Opposite:
Reeds and Lake in Connemara – a magical and mysterious landscape that can conjour up visions of long ago and far away.

Below:
Fairies dancing around a dolmen. It can be seen why they can be called the "little army", betraying their presence only by the dust they threw up when they were on the march.

Doon Hill, Aberfoyle, Perthshire, the fairy
haunt where the Reverend Robert Kirk was
believed to have been taken into fairyland at
his death in 1692.

recorded as recently as 1604, in south-west England pixies, in other parts of Britain brownies. These were not the fairy folk of the ancients. For those who were afraid of fairies, the answer was the herb rue, which the fairies hated, and often rue was kept in a house to keep the fairy folk away.

In mythology fairies were unpredictable and could be mischievous, friendly, or hostile. King Conary, a great warrior, had been battling and could go on no more until he quenches his thirst. He sends one of his men to find water. The man scours Ireland, from the great well of Kesair in Wicklow to the great rivers, but the fairy folk have sealed the sources of water against him. In fact, as he approaches the wells, lakes ands rivers disappear. Eventually he finds a lake, Loch Gara in Roscommon, which failed to hide itself in time. He fills his cup, returns to the king, but too late, finding two of the enemy in the process of lopping off the king's head. He kills them, and taking up the head pours water into the king's mouth. The head thanks him and praises him.

In one story the fairies are indeed "wee folk". The royal bard of the wee folk announces to his king that there is a giant race overseas in a land called Ulster, one man of which would annihilate a whole battalion of the wee folk. The king sends

Holy well, the Burren, County Clare. These provided magic refreshing and life-saving water to the gods and heroes, except for King Conary, for whom the sources of all water were dried up by the fairies. This particular holy well is alleged to cure toothache.

Stones, as with all inanimate objects, could be endowed with supernatural powers, especially if they were associated with St. Brigid, who was evolved from the pagan goddess Brigid or Brigit.

Right:
Fairies often had specific roles to play. This wood nymph was painted by the great Pre-Raphaelite artist, Edward Burne-Jones

him to prison for his impudence, and the bard is only released
when he promises to prove his claim. In due course he goes to
King Fergus, and is borne in upon the hand of the king's
dwarf Aeda. After wining and dining the wee bard returns
home with Aeda, who is regarded as a Fomorian giant, and
the wee folk flee. The king, realising he has been wrong, and
therefore under a geis or ritual duty, is obliged to go to King
Fergus and taste the king's porridge, taking with him his wife.

They arrive by magic steed at midnight, and the wife decides
it would be better to break in, eat the porridge as promised,
and leave immediately. The porridge-pot is too large, and the
king falls in, and when Fergus's servants find him, with his
wife lamenting, they take him to the king, who is amazed by
the appearance of yet another wee creature (with wife as well),
and although he is hospitable he refuses to let them go.

The wee folk arrive in a multitude and ask for their king's
release, but Fergus refuses, so the wee folk visit the country
with various plagues, snip off the ears of corn, let the calves
suck the cows dry, defile the wells, etc., but the king remains
unconvinced.

They therefore change their stance, and in their role as
earth-gods they promise Fergus that the plains before the
palace will be thick with corn every year without sowing or
ploughing. Eventually Fergus relents, if the wee folk let him

have the cauldron which can never be emptied, the harp that plays itself, and magic shoes enabling the wearer to go on, in, or over water, a mythological skate-board.

However, the wee folk, probably feeling that all in all they have not got out of it too well, have not finished with Fergus yet. Fergus has a habit of exploring lakes and rivers, but on one expedition he encounters the hideous sea-monster, the Muirdris, which occupies one of the lakes. Fergus escapes, but the shock twists his face in a ghastly fashion, and as a blemished king cannot hold office the queen and the nobles hide all the mirrors. One day he strikes one of his servants with a switch for negligence, and she tells him that it would be better to avenge himself on the sea-monster than "do brave deeds on women", and that his face is awry.

He obtains a mirror, sees that the servant is right, and goes out wearing his magic shoes to slay the sea-monster, which he does, and as he slices off the head his face returns to normal. He throws the head of the monster onto dry land, and sinks, presumably to drown, though it was such a good and relatively coherent story that probably the many story-tellers resurrected him for future adventures.

Conan ma Morna, Conan the Bald also fell foul of the fairy folk. Conan the Bald is not to be confused with Conan mac Lia, who was Finn's successor with the Fiana, and who served him faithfully for thirty years. But name-confusions are commonplace in the genre.

Conan was not only bald, but big, unwieldy, gross, with a bitter and scurrilous tongue. He was also unutterably greedy. One day out hunting they came across a stately building, white-walled, with coloured thatch, and they entered it to seek hospitality. There was no one in, but they found a marvellous hall hung with silk and with pillars of cedar wood. On a table was set forth a meal of boar flesh and venison, with a yew vat full of red wine, and cups of gold and silver.

They gorged themselves, until one of the number suddenly noticed that the tapestried walls were changing to rough wooden beams, the ceiling to sooty thatch, and that the room was shrinking and by the time they reached the door - all except Conan who was still eating and drinking - the door was no bigger than a the opening of a fox earth.

They realised that it was the work of the fairy folk. Some of them got out, Conan was stuck to the chair with lime, and two of his companions, seeing his dilemma, tugged at him, leaving most of his clothes and his skin sticking to the chair. They looked around and saw the skin of a black sheep, which they clapped on his back. And there it remained for ever. There does not seem any reason why Conan should be singled out, except that he was obnoxious. Mythology is not necessarily devoid of moral judgements.

It is impossible to over-estimate the power of the standing stones, often situated, as here, near Rossnowlagh, County Donegal, in awe-inspiring isolation.

THE DRUIDS AND AFTER

The importance of the Druids in Irish mythology simply cannot be overestimated, and despite the presence of free-lance story-tellers they exerted an immense influence on what was eventually written down. Their culture was entirely oral, it being against their deepest principles to have anything written down, even at a time when they would have been skilled in Latin or a version of Latin, though the Romans declared that when anything had to be written down by the Druids, as, for example, accounts, it was in Greek.

The word itself is believed to have come from dru-vid, meaning very knowing, wise, and it is from the Romans that we first hear of them, especially from Julius Caesar who in his accounts of his own fightings and adventures has proved to be utterly reliable and free from all idle speculation, important when any aspect of Irish mythology is considered.

Caesar was mainly concerned with the Celts in Gaul but there is every reason to believe that the Druids' role in Ireland was exactly the same. All men of substance were included amongst the Druids or the nobles; the Druids were the learned and priestly class, and were the chief enforcers and guardians of the law, an elite with great powers, though some Roman writers dismiss them somewhat contemptuously as merely bards and soothsayers.

The Druids were believed to be able to render people insane by flinging a magic wisp of straw in their faces, to be able to create the clouds of mist so common in Irish myths or bring down showers of blood or fire. They possessed the ability to forecast the future by watching the clouds, could confer invisibity on whom they chose, and had various and peculiar means of divination.

One of the greatest penalties the Druids could impose was excommunication from society, and many of the myths concern heroes or demi-gods forced into an exile, though often the reasons are cosmic rather than by decree. The Druids were held in awe, understandably, and it might be inviting retribution to discuss their actions, though they do feature in the mythology, often sharing their appointed positions in society with poets.

Previous page:
Stone circle, Drombohilly Upper, County Kerry, silhouetted against the sky.

Right:
Grania, daughter of Cormac the High King, questions an old Druid about times to come. Grania falls in love with Dermot of the Love Spot, a great friend of Finn. Finn, then an old man, is to wed Grania, but she elopes with Dermot. Dermot is killed, and she returns to the Fiana, who mock her, and declare that they would not have given one of the dead man's fingers for twenty such as Grania.

Above:
Druids in conference in their sacred groves of oak.

GRANIA QUESTIONS THE DRUID

Unlike the nobles, they were not a hereditary class, and enjoyed exemption from otherwise compulsory service as a warrior. They were also free of taxes. Not surprisingly admission to the order was eagerly sought by the young, but many tried and few were chosen. The training could take twenty years, and nothing could ever be written down. The president of the order, who was elected, served for life, and enjoyed absolute authority over all the other Druids.

The Druids taught that the soul was immortal, and astrology, geography, physical science and natural theology were among their specialist skills. The Romans accused them of human sacrifice, and forbade their citizens - for when they occupied a country whether it was Gaul or Britain the inhabitants automatically became Roman citizens - to practise their rites and customs. The Druids became too much of a threat and were suppressed, but they continued their religion, if religion it can be called, in secret. The Druids revered the mistletoe, and groves of oak were their chosen retreat, though when there was danger they retreated to caverns and the depths of the forest.

Oak was a sacred tree, whatever grew from it was considered a gift from heaven, and when mistletoe was found it was cut with a golden knife by a white-clad priest, and two white bulls were sacrificed on the spot.

The Druids were largely driven from England and Wales after a battle in Anglesey, where the Roman soldiers were struck with awe as the Druids, hands uplifted, hurled imprecations at them. But the Romans remustered, and put the Druids to flight, cutting down the sacred oak groves of what was then called Mona. But in Ireland, untouched by Roman law, they flourished.

They are mentioned in the story of Etain, the wife of a high-king of Ireland, who in a former existence was loved by the god

Druids haranguing their disciples amidst the sacred groves.

Mider. He carries her off, and the king confers with the Druid Dalän who finds the errant couple with the aid of four wands of yew inscribed with Ogam characters (Ogam was a form of Latin). One of the Druid's duties was to act as intermediaries between gods and mortals, as we had seen in the myth of Cuchulinn and the draught-inducing oblivion.

The origin of Druidism is simply not known, and certainly pre-dates the arrival of the Celts in Ireland. Nothing in the mythology accounts for their existence; they are just there, an intimidating real presence amongst the monsters, ogres, gods and demi-gods, though, such is the nature of Irish mythology, that there may be in-built clues in the various "strange and senseless" stories.

That Druidism existed is certain. The cult is still carried on in the Celtic fringes of Britain, though this must not be confused with the Order of Druids, a friendly society founded as an imitation of the ancient order in London in 1781, adopting Masonic rites, and spreading to America in 1833.

If the origins of Druidism are unknown, what do we know of the early history of Ireland and does it correspond in any way

Ogam (or Ogham) stones, representing from left to right February (willow), Earth (beech) and Water (poplar), hanging at Monasterboice in Ireland. Although a language with a relationship to Latin, Ogam was used sparingly, on wooden staves or on stones.

with the myths? The traditions of the Irish people are the oldest of any race in Europe north and west of the Alps, and they are the longest settled on their own soil.

There is no doubt that in pre-history Ireland was peopled by neolithic men, users of flint, indistinguishable from the ancient peoples of other countries. They existed, left unexplained stones and dolmens (two upright stones with one across the top, probably initially covered with earth, certainly burial chambers and reckoned the abode of the fairy folk), and were superceded rather than conquered by more sophisticated races, first of all short dark people from the Mediterranean who may correspond with the Firbolgs of myth and legend. Later Scotland and Northern Ireland were populated by the Picts, skilled in bronze, known in Irish as the Cruithne. This probably explains why a good deal of the mythological action takes place in Ulster. Then about 350 BC came the Celts from the centre of Europe, the warlike people who ransacked Rome and provided a tremendous threat to the civilizations of the Mediterranean. The Celts were tall, red-blond of hair, and spoke a species of Latin. The Gaelic Celts came direct from southern France and northern

Above:
Julius Caesar and the Romans were contemptuous of the Druids, regarding them as unimportant soothsayers, and they were driven out of mainland Britain in a great battle at Mona (Anglesey).

Left: An Ogam stone, Dunmore Head, County Kerry.

Spain and conquered Ireland; the British Celts came from France and the areas by the mouth of the Rhine and conquered the mainland of Britain. Britain and Ireland were the last conquests of the Celts as Rome became supreme.

The Celts were warlike, aristocratic and masterful, destined to be the political masters of Ireland, but an upper-class minority as late as AD 800. They inherited a great body of myths, the Tuatha and Firbolg legends, and to these they added their own, so that we get a stylistic mix, making straightforward stories extremely complicated.

Ireland was full of sacred places, the burial mounds - the abode of the fairy folk, the sacred groves of the Druids, the sacred wells, pillar stones, and the great hill fortresses such as Tara, Emain Macha, and Aileach. Monarchy became the form of government, though on the continent the Celts were republican. Ireland was already divided into "fifths" or kingdoms, and

Left:
Mistletoe growing on an apple-tree and not an oak. When found, the Druids cut it off with silver knives and oxen were sacrificed on the spot. Used to induce love, fertility and health, it was also effective in repelling demons.

Right:
Rock Close, a magical area in the grounds of Blarney Castle associated with the Druids, so much so that some of the ancient stones are said to be petrified Druids. The Blarney Stone nearby, although of antiquity in itself, gave those who kissed it the gift of the gab (blarney) only in recent times.

these province-kingdoms were divided into petty states called Tuatha, of which by about AD 1000 there were probably a hundred or so.

The religion was of course Druidism, and some authorities maintain that this was brought to Ireland by the Celts, though the facts, what there are, seem to be against this theory. Certainly the Celts modified Druidism. The written language was Ogam, but not "literary", and is largely known through funeral descriptions on upright stones or terse passages of writing on wooden staves.

An institution of the Celts was their learned class, the "Filí", poets or seers, whose functions overlapped some of those of the Druids, so much so that it is difficult to differentiate between

103

Until they were ejected by the Romans, the Druids held sway over south-western England. The boy on Glastonbury Tor in Somerset represents the new age. The illustration is by Horace Knowles for A. G. Chant's *The Legend of Glastonbury* (1948).

them. They helped preserve the traditions, the legends, pedigrees, and the history of the race, trying to sort out the truth from a mass of contradictions.

When Christianity came - theoretically with the arrival of St Patrick in 432 but certainly earlier through wandering bands of monks, returned colonists from Wales and Britain who had been converted, and British slaves whose Christian beliefs were taken over by their masters - the Celts adapted to the new faith without problems, blending Christianity with their old beliefs, sometimes giving the ancient heroes a veneer of respectability by turning them into knights who had a probity largely unknown in ancient mythology, and who sometimes had a Christian remit - such as the search for the Holy Grail in Arthurian legend (which may have originated in Ireland but was certainly widespread anyway).

Druidic sacrifice. Much of the savagery blamed on the Druids was a later gloss, perpetuated in the cause of Christianity or to make the storytellers' tales more gruesome. The Druids were not a monstrous elite, but the scholars and lawgivers of the ancient peoples of Ireland.

During the early days of the Celts, the subject peoples, equated with the Firbolgs, were often rebellious, but as the Celts exerted their authority with unquestioned ease there was little that they could do except succumb. In AD 100 they did rebel, but it was crushed with no great effort, and they never tried it again. Meath and Connaught (called Connacht) were united, and formed for centuries a central High Kingship. In AD 200 the country was divided into two parts, with the spheres of influence of the rulers running along a ridge of sandhills from Dublin to Galway.

The king of the south was Eoghan Mór, also known as Mogh Nuadat (devotee of the god Nuada, who features in mythology). There were constant battles and continuous rivalry, and one of the great names of around AD 300 was Cormac , who was one of the most important nation-makers, and who made Tara's

105

Above:
Druidic sickle, a detail of *Country Magic* (1984), a painting by Gordon Wain.

Right:
Cormac's Chapel, Cashel, though the architecture is evidently that of a period later than King Cormac, one of the most illustrious of the Celtic heroes.

Left:
The mystery and legends of the Druids have led to them being transmuted into many fields. Here in the so-called *Esoteric Tarot* the Druid card was used instead of the Emperor card in standard layouts.

ancient and sacred hill the capital of his Ireland.

On its broad green summit was a great banqueting place and the timber halls of kings, princes and nobles. Every three years a great feast was held, a national assembly for law and administration with music, games, and a literary contests. At a time when Rome was moving from central stage and was soon to lose all power to prevent the approach of the Dark Ages, the Irish became the upholder of European civilization, and had a basic unity, despite occasional wars and squabbles (which were probably regarded as hardly more than tournaments) that lasted until the Norman conquest.

Cormac created a network of five great roads traversing his kingdom, and developed a standing army, the Fiana of mythology, the chief of which was Finn, of whom we have already heard. Finn, even after he was crushed when it was considered he was over-reaching himself, became one of the great national heroes of Ireland, immediately incorporated into legend and given supernatural powers, as were his son, the poet Oisin, his grandson Oscar, and Diarmid.

One of the greatest rulers and hero-figures of this time was Niall, who reigned from Tara from 380 to 405, tall, fair-haired, blue-eyed, and from him descended the O'Donnells and the O'Neills. Constant attacks were made by Niall and his successors on the mainland of Britain and for a time the Irish held the west coast. It seemed likely that they would occupy both Wales and Scotland with the withdrawal of the Roman army, and in the event their influence upon Scotland was permanent. The Scots of Ireland, in fact, gave Scotland its name. As a later book has it, in the fifth and sixth centuries "great was the power of the Gaels (Irish) over the Britons, and they divided the isle of Britain between them, and not more numerous were the Gaels at home than those who dwelt in Britain." This statement is perhaps over-emphatic.

107

THE COMING OF ST. PATRICK

The arrival of Ireland's national saint transformed the country. St. Patrick was a Roman Briton of sixteen, captured by the Irish on one of their raids, who escaped from slavery six years later, made his way to Britain and then to Gaul where he studied and became a priest. There was great urgency to convert Ireland for there was fear that its paganism would contaminate Roman and Christianized Britain, but the first priest nominated suddenly died, and Patrick was consecrated bishop and despatched, centering himself in north-east Ulster where a local prince presented him with the site of a church at Armagh. Still a holy place to be reckoned with.

Although there was initial opposition from the ruling classes, it was not acrimonious. St. Patrick was not converting a heathen nation, but a highly cultivated and sophisticated race. He did not work alone; he had plenty of helpers from Gaul and Britain, and was soon able to recruit from the more suitable and amiable of the local people who may have become more fervent than he was. New converts are often the most aggressive and uncompromising. St. Patrick carefully shaped the new Irish church so that it co-existed with the pagan past, and St. Patrick often features in the mythology of the time.

The worship of the sun was one of the staple features of the old mythology, and St. Patrick diplomatically termed Christ sol verus - the true sun. Heliolatry (sun-worship) was accommodated within Christianity, and there is evidence in the majestic high crosses of ancient times, still proudly standing in not only Ireland but what was Celtic Britain, in which the cross is surrounded by a circle (or halo), to make a wheel, the symbol throughout the mythologies of the world of the sun. The Celtic cross is an expression of the rare ability of pagan and Christian religion not only to exist side by side but reinforce each other.

Naturally there were those of the old hereditary order who refused to have anything to do with Christianity, even when it was made pliable - though sometimes obliquely sinister - by St. Patrick, and there were nobles who insisted on being buried upright in the traditional manner. But many of the high-born were

Previous page:
Slane Monastery, County Meath, founded by St. Patrick in 433. The arrival of Christianity transformed Celtic life, and, despite the best efforts of Rome and zealous bishops, Christianity and the ancient religions managed to co-exist.

Right:
Bective Abbey, County Meath. Without great centres of population, many substantial abbeys were set amidst endless rolling pasture. This would have been impossible had there been a hostile aggressive aversion to the new ways.

Below:
St. Patrick's bell-case. Irish bells were rectangular, like Swiss cow-bells.

converted, and Christianity initially prospered, though there was a lapse into paganism after St. Patrick's death, and the Druids, who had seen their powers ridiculed or drained away, re-established themselves, though they too would be, even if unconsciously, including Christian elements in their doctrines.

The structure of the Irish church, so remote from Rome and the strictures of the Pope, was complicated, with lay and spiritual powers inextricably mixed. Many of the dioceses conveniently coincided with the territories of the ancient tribal states. The converted noble who gave lands to the church could find that he had also given his rights, including servants, tenants, and vassals. The recipient (or coarb - co-heir) had the right to exact duties and tributes like other chieftains, even the right to wage war. Such was the organization of the Irish church that abbots could be in subjection to bishops.

The abbot of Louth, supposedly a disciple of St. Patrick, had a hundred bishops in his "monastic family." There were consequently a huge number of bishops without dioceses, who, with the multitude wandering scholars, emigrated to Britain and the continent. Many established centres of learning throughout the Dark Ages. Without them Britain and parts of Europe would probably have reverted to barbarism as the Roman occupation had expunged the civilization that had existed before.

With a host of scholars and clergy meandering through Ireland,

Passage graves, Carrowkeel, County Sligo, which must have appeared as mysterious to the newcomers as they were magical to the local people.

112

Stone beehive huts in County Kerry. The Celts were skilled bee- keepers from the earliest of times, not only for the making of nutritious honey but the production of mead (fermented honey with water) the great alcoholic drink of ancient times. Many of the monks became adept in the craft, a skill that persists in many abbeys (such as Buckfast Abbey, Devon).

together with the professional story-tellers, and men inculcated into the traditions of Druidism, the myths of Ireland, sometimes interlaced with definite Christian elements, were told time and time again.

A charming story in which pagan and Christian features intermingle is concerned with the spell of harp music. The Fomorians, the forces of evil, who in this instance could fly, captured the harpist of the Dagda and carried him off with them. Lug and a warrior named Ogma followed them and gained entrance to the banqueting hall of the Fomorian camp, where they saw the harp hanging on the wall. The Dagda called to it and immediately it flew off the wall into his hands, killing nine Fomorians on the way.

"Come, apple-sweet murmerer," the Dagda cried, "come, four-angled frame of harmony, come, summer, come, winter, from the mouths of harps and bags and pipes." A mysterious evocation, but oddly enough echoed in other mythologies connected with music. There is an Egyptian legend reported by the English musicologist Dr. Burney in his *History of Music* where the three strings of the ancient lyre were supposed to answer respectively to the three seasons of spring, summer, and winter (in Ireland the year contained only three seasons, with autumn incorporated in summer).

When the Dagda gained possession of the harp he played the

"three noble strains" which every great harpist should command, the Strain of Lament, causing listeners to weep, the Strain of Laughter, making them happy, and the Strain of Slumber, sending them to sleep.

Under cover of the sleeping Fomorians the Dagda escaped. This is a prelude to the story, showing how great the power of music was (and is) to the Irish. In *The Colloquy of the Ancients*, probably recorded for the first time in the thirteen or fourteenth century, St. Patrick is introduced to a minstrel, Cascorach, a handsome curly-headed dark-browed young man, who played so appealingly that the saint and his retinue fell asleep. St. Patrick's scribe remarked that it was good. St. Patrick said "Good indeed it were, but for a twang of the fairy spell that infests it; barring which nothing could more nearly resemble heaven's harmony." A back-handed compliment, no doubt, but well intentioned. Some of the most beautiful of Irish melodies, the core of which still haunt the Irish tunes of today, are held to have been overheard by mortal harpists at the revels of the fairy folk.

The tale of Ethné also involves St. Patrick. Ethné was a lovely and gentle maiden, even though she took no nourishment of any

Above:
St. Patrick's statue, Croagh Patrick, County Mayo.

Right:
An ornate and splendid cross seven metres high, said to date back to the tenth century. The tall round tower at Monasterboice is characteristic of Irish Christian Architecture.

ERECTED BY
JAMES QUINN
CALROOSTOWN IN LOVING
MEMORY OF HIS WIFE
MARY BRIDGET
WHO DIED JAN. 21ST 1941,
AND HIS MOTHER LIZZIE
DIED MARCH 9TH 1919, ALSO
HIS FATHER MICHAEL

Upper Lake Glendalough Co. Wicklow.
The spirit of Ireland displayed in a glorious
profusion of shade and light.

kind. The rest of the household fed on the magic swine, which
were eaten one day and were alive again for the next meal.
Mananan, the god of the sea who often seems like a multi-pur-
pose god, was called in to investigate. The story came to light.
Someone had taken a fancy to Ethné and had tried to rape her.
This aroused in her moral repulsion of a kind not known to the
gods, whose morals were at least suspect, and her "guardian
demon" left her and the angel of the true Christian god took its
place. She did not need food, Mananan and Angus (Ethné's foster parent) went to the East, and brought back two cows whose
milk never ran dry and as the cows were supposed to have come
from a sacred place Ethné lived on this milk.

This all took place in the distant past, and by the time St.
Patrick arrived Ethné was 1500 years old, though her people
grew from childhood to maturity and then remained so, without
further signs of age. At this point in the saga it seems uncertain
whether Ethné is human or a supernatural being. Ethné clearly

The Little Skellig, seen from Skelling Michael,
off the west coast of Ireland, a traditionally
sacred place.

Detail of the magnificent cross in Monasterboice, with its medley of interlacing abstract and naturalistic forms.

was not one of the upper echelons of society, for she appears to have been a handmaiden to a princess. They went down to the River Boyne to bathe, and Ethné discovered that she had lost her veil of invisibility, which gave her entrance to the fairyland and hid her from mortal eyes.

Completely lost, she tried to find her way back home, and came to a walled garden. Looking through the gate she saw a man in a long brown robe, who turned out to be a monk. He beckoned her into the church, and when she had told her story to him he took her to St. Patrick, who confirmed her now human status by giving her the rites of baptism. These also meant that she was irretrievably divorced from any association with her own kind.

One day she was praying and heard a rushing sound in the air coupled with innumerable voices lamenting and calling her name, her people still searching for her. She sprang up to reply but was so overcome with emotion that she fainted, recovered

119

Left:
The High Cross of Castledermot, outstanding through its hectic profusion of human forms, often aligned in groups as in traditional medieval church building, mingled with the characteristic swirling Celtic motifs, unique to the race.

Right:
Flying to baptism and the sanctuary of the church from the looming figure of the grim reaper, a startling image from 1899.

for a while, but was then struck with a fatal sickness, dying with her head on the breast of St. Patrick who administered the last rites and ordained that the church should be called Kill Ethné. The syllable "kill" was often used in Irish place-names, such as Kilkenny, Killine and Kilcooley, and comes from the Latin cella, a monastic cell, shrine or church. Pathetic as the story is, it seems that Ethné had rather a poor deal.

One of the most dramatic portrayals of the supernatural powers of St. Patrick was recorded in the twelfth-century *Book of the Dun Cow*, which also reveals that although there was a certain amiability between pagans and Christians this did not mean that the pagans were spared the terrors of Hell. The ancient hero Cuchulinn, who in early sagas enjoyed the never-ending delights of the Otherworld, was summoned from Hell by St. Patrick to report back on the horrors of damnation to a pagan monarch, Laery mac Neill. With a companion the king is standing on a plain when a blast of icy wind nearly takes them off their feet. St. Benen, a companion of St. Patrick, explains that this is the wind of Hell, opened up for Cuchulinn to emerge. And emerge he does, dressed in the splendour of a warrior, in a huge phantom chariot with two horses, a grey and a black.

He entreats the king to mend his ways, recounting all his heroic deeds to prove who he is or was, and apparently succeeded in getting the king to relinquish his past and embrace Christianity.

121

Evocative remains of a lost culture near Slea Head, at Dingle.

Overleaf:
St. Patrick's statue, Croagh Patrick County Mayo.

Cuchulinn was not having an easy time of it. The devil had crushed him "with one finger into the red charcoal."

We here touch on the dilemma of the Irish and the arrival of St. Patrick. The threat of hell and damnation was real and believed in, and was a central feature of the Christian church until the age of reason in the eighteenth century. The Otherworld of the old religion was infinitely preferable to the chance of going to hell and the certainty of having to go through purgatory, and there is no doubt that some of the mythology was dreamed up by the Irish church, to emphasize the repercussions of not being a Christian. And there was no better way to scare the ordinary Irishman and Irishwoman than have the great Cuchulinn, perhaps the most charismatic of the ancient figures, in Hell.

It could be that these legends were created shortly after St. Patrick's mission. St. Patrick, as is evident from his autobiography, was well versed in Irish mythology, and as the Pope's representative it was his duty to get converts by any method. These legends could well have been counter-productive and could explain why, after St. Patrick's death, there were was a widespread reversion to paganism, despite, or because of, the efforts of his successors.

Another myth concerns St. Patrick and the heroic Finn. Finn and six companions were hunting in the north and aroused a beautiful fawn, which they chased all day until it disappeared underground. Night came, followed by snow and a heavy storm, and while seeking shelter Finn and his friends came across a palace, which is actually a fairy palace and does not exist in the here-and-now world of Finn, where they gained admittance. They found themselves on a spacious hall with twenty-eight warriors and twenty-eight maidens, one of them playing the harp. After Finn and his men had been feasted it was explained to them that their hosts, who are fairy folk, are in battle with another faction, that three times a year they fight on the green before the mansion, and that each of the twenty-eight warriors had once a thousand men each, but now they were the only survivors. The fawn Finn and his band had chased was one of the maidens in disguise, who had enticed the warriors to help the beleaguered twenty-eight in the battle, which lasts all night.

Finn and his companions are in their element, and triumph, slaughtering a thousand, the casualties they themselves have being healed by magical herbs. There is more fighting and further adventures in the Otherworld, and after a year Finn and his friends rejoin their fellows, presumably human.

The story is narrated by the closest companion of Finn, Keeta, and as he talks, standing on the spot where the fairy palace was, a young warrior approaches; a shirt of royal satin is next to his skin, over that is a tunic of the same material, and he wears a

Left:
Beltany stone circle, near Raphoe, County Donegal, the majestic stones touched by the rays of the moon.

fringed crimson mantle, fixed with a bodkin of gold on his chest. He has a gold-hilted sword and a golden helmet and is one of the twenty-eight helped by Finn; he has come to do homage to St. Patrick.

In this story from *The Colloquy of the Ancients*, of which there are about a hundred tales dealing mostly with fighting and love-making, usually between Finn's people and the fairy folk, St. Patrick is the paternal figure, not the evangelist, as he is also in another amiable story featuring Keelta. In this Keelta is making his way across the plains where he encounters St. Patrick and his monks, who see the band draw near "and fear fell on them before the tall men with the huge wolf-hounds that accompanied them, for they were not people of one epoch or of one time with the clergy."

In other words, Finn and his fellows, despite many stories which establish them as down-to-earth Irish warriors, are as supernatural as the fairy folk. St. Patrick sprinkles the heroes with holy water, and the demons that hover over them fly off. As the sagas have it, St. Patrick has a boon to crave; he wants to find a well of pure water to baptize converts. So Keelta takes St. Patrick on a guided tour, in which St. Patrick says that although it impaired the devout life, made him neglect prayer, and conversation with God was difficult to fit in, time passed quickly, and "Success and benediction attend thee, Keelta!"

Above:
Celtic spiral stones, amulets with supernatural powers, hanging above the great cross at Monasterboice.

Right:
Gortavern portal tomb, Carrowkeel County Sligo.

There is no finer example of the art of illuminated manuscripts than *The Book of Kells*, now housed at Trinity College, Dublin. It was created by the monks of Kells in County Meath in the eighth century.

This is a far cry from his summoning of Cuchulinn from Hell, and once again we have the glaring lack of consistency in Irish mythology, and the abilities of the story-tellers to angle any saga at any audience one cared to think of.

Compared with other Christian formations, St. Patrick's regime was lax. There was no emphasis at all on celibacy. Seeking a bishop for Leinster he asked for a man of one wife; so evidently polygamy was commonplace. After St. Patrick's death, the influences for a "purer" Christianity came from Wales, the leading figure being Findian of Clonard (c. 470 - 548), who introduced the type of monastery with which the great Dark Age civilization of Ireland is associated. He founded his great monastery at Clonard in County Meath about 520, and it is said that no less than 3000 students received instruction at the same time.

The monastery was not one great building, but a huge collection of wattle and clay huts or, where stone was available, cells in the shape of a beehive. The whole was enclosed by a ditch or battlements. Much of the learning was conducted out of doors, and the monastery was self-sufficient, with the students sowing corn, fishing, milking cows, and making their own clothes. Twelve of Findian's followers became the twelve apostles of Ireland, who founded the great seats of learning. There was influence from Britain too; the Irish monasteries were fairly easy-going, but later sexes were segregated and the monastic communities were entirely separate from the ordinary people. They were an elect, and as the years went by this was more and more clear.

The Irish went forth, establishing churches on tiny Scottish islands, and sending what can be seen as missionaries deep into Europe. As for Ireland itself, almost nothing is known between the arrival of St. Patrick and the occupation of Dublin by the Norse four centuries later. There were intertribal rivalries, well represented in myth, and although there was a high king he does not seem to have kept his unruly nobles in order. Tara itself, a place of legend and mystery, was probably deserted during a plague in 548-549. There is little that confirms the myths, little that contradicts them. All is turmoil and strife. There is sound but not sense. We know that there were joint kingships, but hardly why.

Although Tara had been recognized as the capital of all Ireland, when it was left to moulder and decay there was no other town to take its place. It is impossible to determine the role of the travelling scholars and wise men, except that some of them were mischievous and delighted in alarming and frightening the native population; they have been described as impudent and swaggering, quartering themselves on the chiefs and nobles during the winter and spring, story-telling, and lampooning and making fun of those who did not give in to their wishes.

With such discord, so little cohesion, fighting as a way of life rather than a way of settling difficulties, it is no wonder that Ireland fell prey to the Vikings. Despite their learned institutions, which seem to have existed in a kind of vacuum, some ideas in Ireland were prehistoric. It was not until 697 that women were forbidden to take part in battle; not until World War II that the

idea was revived. The Vikings came in 795. They were not necessarily braver than the Irish, but they were organized. The Irish fought when they felt like it, and it was considered no disgrace at a battle just to go away. Their "armies" were bands collected together for a short period. They - seeking a parallel in mythology - were like Finn and his bunch of strolling warriors.

At first the Vikings arrived in small parties. Their ships soon sailed up the rivers and fortresses were set up. There were ships on the inland lakes. The Vikings did not act in concert until 820, but when they did they were unstoppable, with their fury directed at the church as well as the civil authorities (what few there were). Armagh, one of the great church centres, was burnt to the ground ten times and ten times rebuilt. To escape from the continuous attacks the Irish monks, taking their precious books, fled the country.

The Irish monks are shadowy figures in an indistinct landscape. They created probably the greatest art work between the masterpieces of classical times and the magnificent cathedrals of more than a thousand years later. This is the absolutely unique *Book of Kells*, found in Kells, County Meath, an illustrated eighth-century manuscript. Kells is a small town, population 2000, but it was here that a monastery was established by St. Columba (c 521 - 597), dissolved in 1551. St. Columba, though his fame is eclipsed by St. Patrick, was an ardent missionary who not only established monasteries in Ireland but set up one at Iona in 563 as a centre for the conversion of Northern Scotland, and was a brave and intrepid traveller among the Picts, many of whom were far more antagonistic to Christianity than the Irish.

Settling Ireland was different from defeating scattered forces. Dublin was established about 840, and Waterford and Limerick appear at about the same time. As the initial wave of the Vikings was broken on the endless plains of Ireland, as they realised that it was better to occupy the coastal stretches and leave the hinterland well alone, many feudal tribes took the opportunity to snatch land off their rivals. There was often more interest in savaging a fellow king than in combining forces against the invader.

In 848 the Danes came; they were known as the black foreigners as distinct from the white foreigners, the men from Norway. As with the Irish they were warriors, and they fought each other as well as the natives. In many ways, they were akin to the Irish. A fight was a fight no matter who the enemy was; the enemy could be a recent ally, and when the battle was over friendship would be resumed as if nothing had happened.

There was intermarriage, leading to the "foreign Irish", the Gallgoidel (from which Galloway comes from), and there was a descent into paganism.

Everything about Ireland was detrimental to trade and commerce; there is no evidence of a home-grown coinage, and foreign luxury items were only sold at great oenachs or fairs held

Life as it was – Heritage Park in Ferrycarrig County Wexford.

133

periodically throughout the country. Only in the coastal towns controlled by the Vikings did commerce thrive - the invaders formed their own mint, and issued their own coinage, and there was a considerable trade with Italy and the Netherlands. It was through these trade links that Ireland itself came into contact with Europe, centuries after their monks had taken the message abroad, and it was through these cultural changes that Ireland ceased to be an oral-based tribal country, with its traditions actually written down, centuries after the arrival of the Vikings, who no doubt appear in the mythology in some guise or other.

The supreme kingdom in Ireland was Dublin. The king exercised control of the under-kings through the country. However, there was rivalry, the Irish were flexing their muscles, and in 901 they captured Dublin and Waterford, but it was a short-lived success.

Hero figures arose who challenged the Vikings - Muirchertach "of the leather cloaks", and we have mention, it seems, of the legendary Cuchullin, who was not particular whether he fought with or against the Norsemen.

What was Ireland itself like in these days? Before the seventh century there were no fences, therefore no artificial demarkation lines. Before the Vikings there were no cities or large towns, there were no stone bridges spanning rivers (stepping stones were used), and the land was mostly forest, meadows, and pasture.

The Irish forests abounded with game, and the red deer, wolves, and the wild boar were common. The Celtic heroes were hunters, as well as fighters.

The forests abounded with game, the red deer, wolves, and wild boar were common.

There were wicker huts of various sizes, usually cylindrical with conical roofs thatched with rushes, and sometimes these huts were surrounded by ramparts or a ditch, sometimes flooded as a protection against marauders. Every room was a separate hut. The more huts the greater prestige of the family.

The palaces of myth were often merely rectangular buildings made from sawn wood. The wheel was known, most often in a solid form; spoked wheels were reserved for chariots. But there were surprising features of rural Irish society in the Dark Ages; beekeeping was highly regarded and brought to a degree of sophistication. Amongst the upper classes, though they too lived in these wicker or sometimes wattle huts, marriage was usually by purchase, and often between close kin, prohibited by the church which made an unsuccessful effort to stamp it out.

Mythological accounts often go to great lengths to describe the dress of the people, often to the disadvantage of the flow of the narrative. The upper class men dressed similarly to a present day Scottish Highlander, the women wore their hair long (as did the men), and both sexes were fascinated by ornament, a characteristic of many savage races, as was the Irish idea of justice, which was retaliation and revenge and nothing much else, as can be seen in the myths.

There were real traditions from earlier, mistier and barely understood days, before the arrival of the Vikings. There were the fairs at Tara, at Telltown and Carman where disputes were settled or not settled, where there was horse-racing, wrestling, and marathon poetry recitals. Women held their own meetings at these fairs, and men were excluded, on pain of death. It was a society which was strange and unpredictable, and immensely vulnerable, and when the Anglo-Normans invaded Ireland in 1169 it was the end of an age and the beginning of the yearning for past glories. The ancient mythology, fact, fiction, and a mixture of the two, were set down for future generations to puzzle over.

AFTERWORD

Irish mythology must surely be the most extraordinary in the world, and many scholars have come to grief on it, finding the lack of system and the built-in contradictions more than they can cope with. It is luminous and vivid, naive and evocative, and we can well imagine the audiences being entranced by the tales of the Dagda, of the various invasions, of the heroes Finn and Cuchulinn. We can also vizualize the narrators, experienced in their trade, able to fuse paganism and Christianity, often bards and poets in the own right, who could build up tension and had perfected the art of timing. We can also sense an air of cynicism; they gave the audience what they wanted, and when it was appropriate, when they had hit on a vein of gold, they elaborated, ad libbing with gusto, driving their audiences (often victims) into paroxysms of terror or delight.

When they were addressing those of the upper classes they seem to have had no qualms in castigating them, lampooning

Previous page:
The imposing Piper Stones, an ancient stone circle in County Wicklow.

Right:
Killadangan standing stones, below Croagh Patrick mountain, County Mayo, once again a reminder of Ireland's long and tumultuous heritage, still largely uncharted despite dedicated research by generations of Irish archaeologists and historians.

Below:
Mysterious stone figures set against a wall on White Island, Fermanagh. Superficially these seem figures akin to those on Easter Island, but closer inspection reveals that the second figure on the left is holding a square bell and a crozier, so they are of Christian times.

them, reducing them to the status of nincompoops, knowing that they were in control and considering that they were, in every way except for status and wealth, immeasurably superior to the men, women, and children they had as a captive audience. No-one knows or will ever know what they said. The men who finally put it all down in writing had hundreds of years of oral tradition to deal with. Each generation had added their contributions, the Christianized story-tellers had transmuted the stories to bring them into line with their beliefs, and where there were contradictions which could not be resolved, the recorders often did not bother to make a reconciliation or, if they did, they tied up the loose ends themselves to make a satisfactory story.

All nations yearn for a past that is vivid and extraordinary. The English have adopted the legend of Arthur, whether it is theirs or not (and the odds are that it is Irish or failing that Welsh), the Norwegians have their marvellous epics of the gods with Thor the god of thunder and Odin; the Germans have the sagas made into powerful music dramas by Wagner. But perhaps only the Greeks and Romans have a mythology that is comparable in scope and variety to that of the Irish.

The Greeks and the Romans have changed out of all recognition. The Athens of today is impossible to reconcile with the Athens of history. But Ireland is still Ireland, a land of lush mystery, with the enigmatic presence of the dolmens, the standing stones, and the burial mounds which, to the present-day inhabitants, are still the homes of the fairies. And Ireland still has no snakes; St. Patrick drove them out. And few disbelieve it.

Right:
One of the most imposing of the ancient burial tombs, at Killybegs, County Donegal. The abode of the "wee folk"? The resting place for the warriors of Finn before they emerge into a new age? Who can say?

Index

PICTURE CREDITS